Thy Paintbrush to Abstracting Images

By

Shavonda Robinson

Published by True Beginnings Publishing.
Copyright 2017.

Thy Paintbrush to Abstracting Images, By Shavonda Robinson. © Copyright 2017. All Rights Reserved and Preserved. No part of this book may be reproduced or transmitted in any form or by any means, electronic or mechanical, including photocopying, recording, or by information storage and retrieval systems or other electronic or mechanical methods, without written permission of the Author with exceptions as to brief quotes, references, articles, reviews and certain other noncommercial uses permitted by copyright law. For permission requests, write to the Publisher, addressed "Attention: Permissions," at the address below.

true_beginnings_publishing@yahoo.com

Formatting, Editing, and all artwork by True Beginnings Publishing. All Illustrations, Cover Art, and text are Copyright Protected.

ISBN-13: 978-0692839690
ISBN-10: 0692839690

Ordering Information:
To order additional copies of this book, please visit Amazon or CreateSpace, at: https://www.createspace.com/6891403

This book is a compilation of works by the Author. All quotes, thoughts, and writings are products of the Author's imagination. Any resemblance to actual events or persons, living or dead, is entirely coincidental. The quotes, thoughts, and writings are copyrighted to the Author and are protected under US Copyright law. Any theft of the Author's work will be prosecuted to the full extent of the law.

Thy Paintbrush to Abstracting Images.
© Shavonda Robinson.
First Printing, 2017.

To Jehovah,
Without you, I would be nothing,
And I owe it all to you in your glory.
Thank you so much, and I will always
Try my best to follow the path you are showing me.
I love you so much.

To my beautiful children,
LaTesha and Teonis.
You inspire me every day to do my best
And never give up on my dreams.
You are the reason I continue to climb
The ladder toward success.
I believe God sent both of you as
A motivation kicker and as a precious gift to me.
I believe in myself much more than I ever did
Since you both entered my world.
You both are my dream;
My two favorite little heartbeats.
You both taught me what it is to feel special
And beautiful.
You helped me realize my talents.
For that I will always be grateful
For the both of you.
You know I love you both to pieces.

Table of Contents

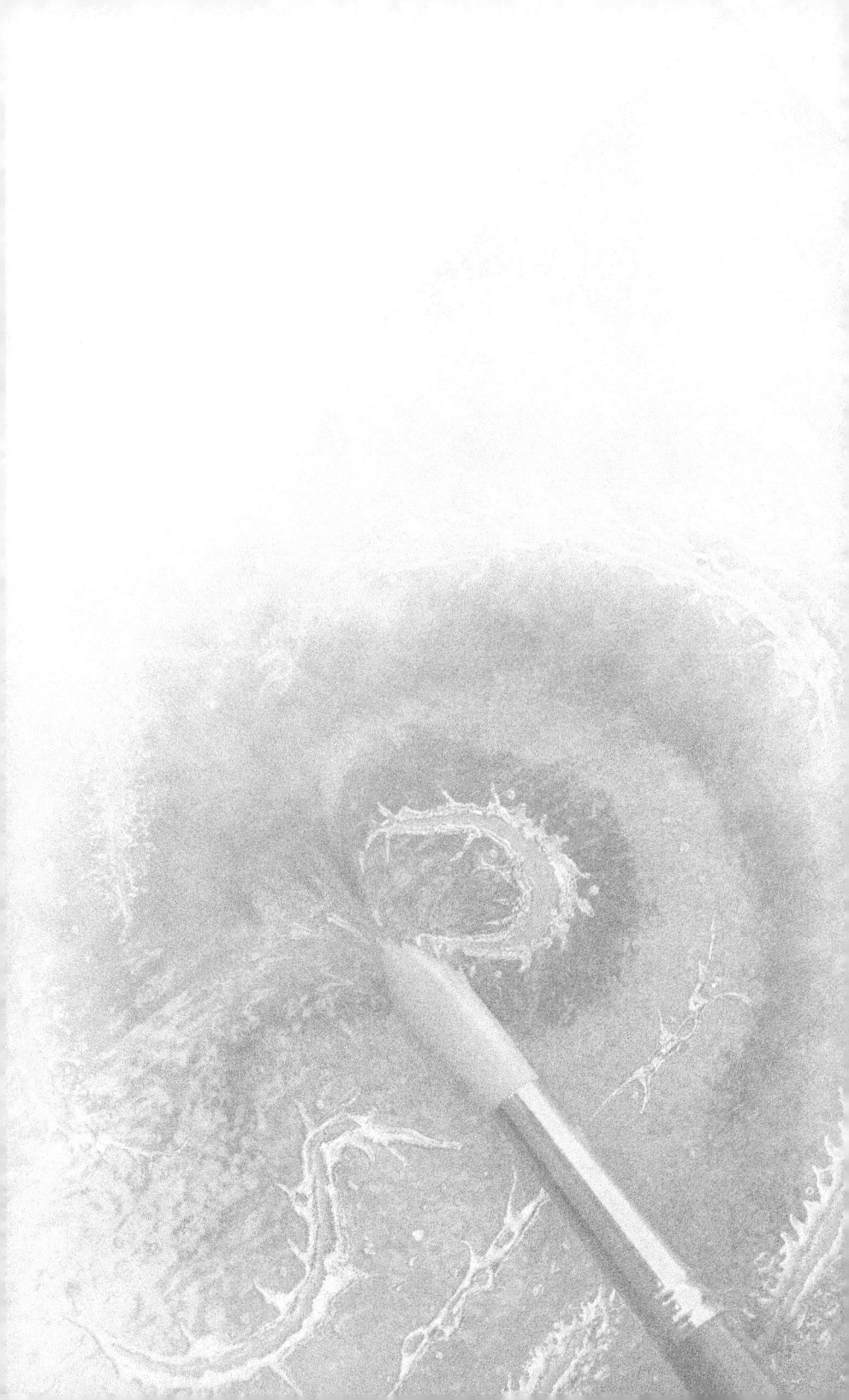

Captivating Taste

Your vision is beautiful.
I am beautiful by your taste.
Different flavors of art,
I can not erase.
Pieces may fall in between
You and I.
I can see your artistic view, faraway.
You are an angel flying away.

Beauty has held me captive for years.
Baby, you got me so addicted
To the colors in you,
Like a rainbow so bright
And full of truth.
Your vision is what led me right to you.
If I could, I would walk through the sea
Just to get to you.

Wanna get lost in your world,
So I can spend my time
Exploring all of you.
Boy, let me tell you,
Your colors shine through.
Different colors of art
Shall lead me to you.

Your vision is beautiful.
I am captivated by your taste.
You are an angel flying away.
I live in forbidden paradise
Where you and I belong together.
I am captivated by your love.
You dare me to fulfill a naughty dream
When I am thinking of you.
Somewhere in a place
Where I can imagine
You and me together
Until the end of time.

Wandering Minds

I have lost my mind.
It wandered off into
The depths of the ocean.
I stand here in question;
When did my mind go missing?
Thoughts have flown to
The bottom of fantasy land.

Common sense flew out to the world,
Saying catch me if you can.
I ran away with my dreams;
I am still searching for it today.
Have you seen my mind?

Floating somewhere out there,
I am pacing all over for you.
Send me a message.
Red light flashing above me,
Wonders flown all over in desperation
To find you.

I have lost my mind.
I shall recover with a shyly smile.
The other part of me
Continues to float in images.
I stand here in question;
When did my mind go missing?
If I watch over things to seek in curiosity,
I have lost my mind; it wandered off into
The depths of the ocean.
Swimming away, you took
My conviction with you.
I will find you.
All I have are a few clues.
Will it lead me to my mind?
So confused.

Singing Languages

Writing is singing
In its own language.
I hear the music.
When it comes to me,
I only despair in words
When I choose to wait on
The meaning of the story.
As a quiet girl once said,
Silence is a misunderstood disease
That is part of us.
We are introvert voices.
Writing is singing in its own language.
Words create such an expression
That is good for our souls.
When it comes to me,
It's so simple-
Poetry seems to find me.
Here I go, catch me
Before I run away into the darkness.
No matter what I do,
Maybe I am defined by the meaning of life
In a depth feeling.

Living outside an empty consciousness,
This is a loss for me.
Elements of surprise remain a
Challenge of who you are.
We are all reaching for the stars.
Writing is singing in its own language.
Writing is the way of the world.

Fixed Thoughts

Fix your thoughts.
Tell me or show me,
Are they false?
Does the truth roam alone
Out somewhere?
Are you an honorable figure
In this weird world?
Pure joy swept you off your feet
To cultivate inner delights.
Showcasing positivity could lead
You on a inspiring path.
Fix your thoughts.
Just waiting to blossom
In its finest hour,
You have the power.
Your heart is beautiful.
Just as teardrops mirror
Your conscious,
Daybreak will come again.
Your hope is greater than love;
Your passion explodes like pleasure.

Your soul is tender and precious;
Someone searching for understanding
Of the world.
This is a visual comparison of images.
It continues to shoot out variety,
Just as teardrops mirror
Your conscious.
Fix your thoughts.
Everything is in sequence.
Images can be gorgeous
From faraway,
Waiting for a word of advice.
Fix your thoughts.
The truth shall be told.
Let things go and they will
Unfold themselves now.

I Enlighten Minds

I enlighten the uneducated minds
Who are blind.
So realistic, like a black woman
With a college degree
Living out her dreams.

We are intelligent.
Open up your minds.
Spoken words with a poetic flow,
My heart tells a story.
Just let it flow.
I love verses; profound ones
Go beyond a foundation of path.

My creative mind draws a picture,
An inspirational path of education.
I enlighten you, still only words can bare.
Those are the words.
Hey, look over there.
You say I am miss uneducated woman
Going nowhere.

Plan a life, plan a future.
To the ones who are blind,
I will shine so uneducated like
No other thirty-two year-old,
Female poetess with a powerful
Generation voice.

I will enlighten you, so listen
To the poetess voice.
Then you will decide
I enlighten minds.

Painted Devotion

We paint on a moving emotion.
I got a potion.
Here is a signed devotion.
When all things move along,
Arising notions create a lyrical masterpiece
To a musical lift.

So clear, my dear,
We watch it all fall down,
Then build itself up again.
How can I pretend?
Do we even know his name?
Hello, Jehovah?

We all have sinned.
We paint on a moving emotion;
Sweet remedy notion
Opens up vibrant calamity.
Pour me into a bright, energetic life.
Take no prisoner.
We are not a shame.
I call on Jehovah to come
Save the day,
Then I pray down on my knees.

Ask him please, for my sanity,
Let me sail away.
We paint on a moving emotion.
His words moved me to tears.
Now, I see this is how
We should be freed of guilt.
A sensation of feeling within
Overcomes me.
Then I start to bleed within me.
I paint on a remedy.
Here comes along devotion.

Timeless Wisdom

Like a beautiful stranger,
Like a beautiful human,
An old, timeless charm
Blows in the air.
We all start to feel
Time and space is missing
As the spaceship comes down
From Mars.
Abducted species talk to me.
Something feels strange;
Our galaxy seems so dizzy.

Raindrops sprinkle from planet
Saturn.
I rode with an alien.
He befriended me;
He took me to a place unfamiliar.
I watched from a distance
As the wisdom continues to
Build on falling charms.
Oddness began raising the bar,
A timeless charm setting ribbons
On a secret mission.

The world we know as space.
We all want to adventure.
I look to the aliens;
My memory, it is shifting
In another position.
We talk, we listen.
Hey, beautiful stranger.
Hey, stranger human.
Time is frozen.
The spaceship is drowning
In the ocean.
Someone, save their lives.
Someone, hear their cries.
All of the aliens from another world
Called out of time.
We can run, but we can't hide.
Look at wisdom taking our pride.
Charms hit me in the head,
Woke me up again,
No one is dead.
Old charm coming along
As the aliens disappear out of sight.

Building Beautiful Words

Those words build a bridge,
I walked over them, creating a beautiful, long poem.
It stood fifty feet into the air with solid words.
I saw it come into something extraordinary
Right before my eyes.
Water surrounded it with a landscape of innovative designs,
Different colors spouting out like fireworks.

Those words are so beautiful to me,
Definitions writing themselves into a segment of art.
I shall be a part of visual eyes.
I walked over the bridge of words.
I captured ideas as they flow into the air;
What color are those words?
The minds they came from
Are open to spare with sparkling details.

I saw the bridge with so many colors
Changing all the time.
Those words built a mile,
And I ran to the nearest sign,
Opening up human minds.
Words build a bridge
Over the shallow water,
While the colors wrote an educational poem.

The bridge of words
Standing over an imagination,
When I was the one who made
The foundation of art.
Standing over there, those words
Are so beautiful as they ring in my ear.
When it comes to me,
I'll be the reader for everyone to see.

Hello, Friend

Hello again, my sorrow friend.
Fairy Tale and folk tales will never end.
I reach out to the sky.
Drifting snowflakes came alive,
Covering the ground in a white blanket.
Fallen sorrow continues on to blame me,
Or am I mistaken?
Pour holy water on my hands.
Let it dry in the sand.

Twist and shake,
Teardrops call on someone's name.
Hello again, sorrow is my friend.
I lend you a helping hand.
I sit down to record my thoughts on paper,
My memories seem as if they want to chase them forever.
No explanation for sorrow,
This is a new era.
Listen to me, listen to me,
Sorrow became a part of me.

When it grabbed ahold of me,
The water drops seemed to flow.
I reach to the sky,
The sorrow falls down like a rainy day.

Look through your eyes,
Can you see me?
It is your friend, sorrow, at the door?
So if I was you, I wouldn't let me in
To take control of you,
My dear friend, sorrow.

God's Avenue Vision

I saw God on the corner of South 4th Street.
He was wearing a white suit and black dress shoes.
I said to him,
"You are here at last!
You are here at last!
You are a real spirit.
Oh, my God, I can really see you
With my own eyes.
Look at you,
Look at me,
Here we are, twirling around in the street
Like playful children."

I said to God
In a peaceful state of mind,
"I need you here with me
To heal me all over again."

Feel the cure beginning to diminish my worries
As God touches me.
My soul of open wounds
Closes up so smoothly.
Where were you
When my life got washed and drained
Like a flooded river?
Just a little late.
Once I tried to take my own life.
Depression drove me to insane avenue.
I parked there for a few hours
But winded up staying forever.
God said to me, "Well, I am here now;
No need to worry."

I saw God on the corner of South 4th Street,
I walked toward him as I began a conversation.
He dried up my tears as they were pouring down
My face.

Then I thought to myself,
He hears my cries.
He knows how I feel, inside and out.
So he came to me; now I feel so cleansed
With a calm inner peace
Buzzing through my body like an electric wire.

I saw God's face; he embraced me with happiness.
I am grateful to have seen you
On the corner of South 4th Street,
Where I was standing all alone,
Shivering in the wintery cold.

God appears out of nowhere.
Here I stand in front of him.
Judgment day arrives on the scene.
He points out to me; all my life sins
Are washed away.
"I said I will erase your wrongdoings.
Get on aboard, and I command you
To be a leader,
Not a follower."
He washed me with buckets of water
From his well; I can tell I am changing in every way.
I saw God on the corner South 4th Street.
He said to me, "Here I am at last."
As he walked on by me into the clouds.

Oceania Thoughts

The ocean writes to me
A personal letter; it is almost like
Someone poured colored dye into the water.
Ocean breeze and fresh surroundings
To be a fairytale dream.

The ocean writes to me,
Telling me to watch
For the horizon sunset
Hiding away its glory.

The ocean mixed it up beyond a potion.
A sweet nursery rhyme
Taught things how to grind.
Juicy watermelon drips from Oceania's mouth of doubt.

Listen, as we are so quiet and shameless,
As the oceans rushes its waves back and forth,
The ocean refuses to dry in land.
When all we see is the vibe,
Making a straightforward void of colorless voices
Run away like someone has escaped.

The ocean writes to me
A long six-paragraph in a note.
I think about its own life
Gliding into the rules of colorful voice.

The ocean writes its thoughts into a letter of understanding,
Pointing toward a map of drifting memories.
A lost breezy wind from the past
Makes you laugh.
The ocean blows a whisper in my ear.
Deep down inside of the bottom,
It is taking on a new life
As the ocean writes to me
In a sign language speech.

I love to watch the deep, beautiful ocean.
I take a snapshot of its own reality.
Oceania speaks to me through eyes
Of its personality.

When the Stars Go Blue

The stars wrap around the universe,
Making them trace in a blessed way.
They all came to say,
We love, we love.
The stars' colors shoot out,
All twelve in a row.
The stars go blue in the dark.

Dancing, prancing, making new stars,
Tracing alphabets as they go.
When the stars go blue,
Lines seem to become more complex, like you.
Stars preach a written verse that I wrote
In a note a long time ago.
The stars shine so bright away from the moon.
Hello, Again!
We all are the stars' true mood
From the distance.

The stars form a view.
They seek all reasons
To be defined by value.
The stars go blue, faraway.
This is another day playing musical chairs.
Where do they stand?

Oh! Look way up there.
Can you tell me the meaning behind superstars?
Because the only stars I see
When I look up in the sky,
Those are the ones who shine so bright.
He has a starring role.
There he goes to shine so brightly again.
Can he catch a wondering star in his hands?
True confessions of strange beauty held within
When the stars go blue.
He imitates them with a black pen on paper.
Take a look at them,
The stars are taking over.
He documents his experience;
Still he wonders why
The stars go blue.
All in a dark shadow,
Wearing the colors white, red, and blue
As the stars go chasing around the moon.

Beautiful Classic

The script in my mind became
A beautiful classic on the road
To a timeless discovery.
The paintings became a visual
Thought to a innovative scene,
Dedicated to the aspiring mainstream.

Beautiful ideas building itself
Into a personal visionary scenery.
The script floats on a cloud with no melody.
Classic notes transforming into shattering instruments.
The script of my mind,
A recreation of the universe
Appeals to the sense of classic
Vision without permission.
This is our decision.

Classic sounds sing a song
As a woman continues to hum along in a low tone.
The scripts start to drown in musical sounds.
Here are the ideas I wrote; a classic Vision,
Thriving on an impact full of creations.

Spiral Eternity

I build the blocks up like a mountain.
Now I stand upon it to watch you
From a distance.
Rising to the top
Marks the birth of a star.
I barely touched the top before falling so hard,
Before I stumble,
Feeling so weak at the knees.

Fainting in a spell,
Oh, Sandy, pour water on me.
Build up a mountain out of blocks,
Starting from all the alphabets,
A through Z.
God, can you see blocks up so high,
Reaching all the way up to heaven.

I stand upon the blocks,
Rising to the top after recovering from a relapse.
Can you see me walking toward
A spiral eternity?
Here are the gods of past history myth.

Counting on fingers awaits a fantasy
Which I stand upon mountains set way back.
I will walk to you, my God,
Elevated by powers to walk on the line
Rising to the top.
I fell to the bottom
Where scars covered up my body,
But I get up and continue to walk on forward
Through the mountains of blocks.

Shavonda Robinson

Words on a Stage

The words came out to take center stage.
Inspiration plays a role in the show.
The words' talent grabs a starring role;
Creation of a script turns into a big hit.

The words jumped out and screamed, "Watch me!"
The words on a stage
Came into a brilliant play.
Words play with each other,
Making the story so colorful.

The words put on a scene,
Speaking a beautiful language.
The words perform in a Broadway show.
The words skip along, singing a song.
Entertainment shows the crowd with its
Words of excitement.

Words sit in the crowd
Applauding themselves on the back.
Jumping words on the stage
Love to perform.
The talented words take a bow
It's over as the stage
Has put on its best show ever.

Lyrical Galaxy

The sky will soon fall down,
But two galaxies still exist.
I spin around, you spin around,
Then we both become dizzy.
Can you reach up in the sky
And grab me a star?

Behind the black sky at night,
I bear music; playing lyrics roll right by me.
I caught them with my voice.
Twinkle, twinkle;
Sorry, I can't be nobody's shining star.

Two different worlds of harmony,
Still the galaxy keeps calling on me.
I pretend I am a ballerina,
Tiptoeing around the galaxy.
Distant humming, I keep hearing music ahead of me;
Someone playing a keyboard.
Harmonizing at the same time,
Music surrounds my ears.
The galaxies still exist, spinning for years.
The sky will fall down someday.
The black sky is fading away.
Sailing on into the darkness of light,
Lyrics become more apparent to me.

Charisma Lady

Raindrops fall in the dark.
See the pianist play a beautiful set,
Wearing her black leather dress.
She's a mysterious queen.
The lady pianist got skills; word of mouth is
She is the hottest thing on the block.
Her fingertips glide like a friendly bird in the sky.

Waving her hands up high,
She swallows her pride.
She takes a pill and turns into someone else;
A character pretending she's an actor.
Excuse me! Miss charisma,
I like your style.
Her beautiful hands light up
The piano in the dark.

Raindrops fall in the dark.
Her interviews feel like confessions
When she's sitting in the spotlight chair.
Kiss and tell or go to jail.
Traces of her lipstick
Draw original pictures in her head.
Like I said, lady in the dark,
You play the piano like a pro.

Lady of dark dream,
Do you hear her voice
Playing the piano?
She sings like an angel on the keys,
Fading away in the night,
So mysterious, feeling like a faraway dream.

Stand up and bow, please!
The stage is where you confide.
Dry your eyes, perform like a midnight stroke.
Let everyone know
You are miss charisma
Running the show.

Scribbling Images

I scribble some images on the walls
Of a vacant building.
I wonder will the world
Think it is beautiful or not?
Scribble, scrabble on a drawing pad.
Somehow ideas turn into an roaming masterpiece.
Abstract designs is a normal
Space filled with traces of ink.
When it comes to an underestimated mind,
Who knows what to think.

Can you see an artistic vision
Expressed across the building's walls?
Are you an artist,
Maybe an undiscovered literary genius?
Illustrated drawings creep across the page
Of her canvas,
Then she paints on buildings;
Hooray to her satisfaction.

Spread the colors across her imagination
Into an empty building.
Scribbling images forces my ego,
Therefore, her expression leaves a lasting
Impression.

When she was scribbling images
On a vacant building,
It leaks out a colorful expression
In her imagination,
Showcasing all imagery onto the building
For everyone to see.
Someone's ideas can turn into
A thing of beauty.
Hooray for satisfaction!
Hooray for satisfaction!

Kid Brilliant

I can see him.
There must be a thousand words
Floating through his head.
No wonder he's
An invisible figure.
He talks to himself
Just a little bit,
But I don't think he is crazy.

The kid is brilliant.
Have you heard him
Talk in a conversation?
Listen to his voice.
I am telling you,
There is something special about him.

Cool personality, if you ask me.
The kid has a brilliant vocabulary
And knowledge to back it up.
Wow! Listen to him,
He is only eight years old.
How did he become so deep?

The kid is on fire,
He got the power to send
Shockwaves across the world.
He is so intelligent.
What do they call you?
Kid brilliant.
Oh yeah, kid brilliant?
Can I shake your hand;
I am your biggest fan.

The kid is brilliant.
I can see him.
There must be a thousand words
Floating through his head.
He's always been a curious kid
As long as I can remember.
He is an intelligent kid
Who is on fire.
He is unbelievable.
Wow, he is a gifted child.

Kid brilliant walks on holy ground.
Turn around, see his smile,
Making silly faces to each other.
He brilliantly speaks with so much
Depth at his age.
You are truly a gift to the world.
He is not an invisible figure to me.
You are a brilliant kid on fire,
Ready to take over the world.
You have a brilliant mind and
An old soul for a youngster.

Capturing Time

So many faces,
So many places,
He climbs the ladder to pureness.
His thoughts are so beautiful.
There's a sand castle in the sky.
He smells the sweet blue tulips.
The thorns are so sharp,
They cut his hand,
And he bleeds out romance.

He stands in the sand.
Magic touches the air.
Beauty arises in the emotions.
His potential builds an empire
More than images can imagine.
He stands on top of the castle,
Talking to a nearby passenger.
A bush of tulips
Is a wife's favorite flower.

He takes a photo of the sand castle
Across the world.
He tours the country,
Drinking a bottle of whiskey in his hands.
He asks some lady to dance.
Only if he could capture time in a bottle
And send it floating down the ocean.
The message receives no notion.

He sails the boat away.
Come on, can we stay?
Let's say amazing grace.
He stands on top of the castle,
Taking a lifetime of photos,
Enjoying the moment sinking in motion.

Dancing in the Distance

She is a dancing sunflower;
So big, so bright, so beautiful.
The tones of her colors
Are so striking to the eyes.
The tone of her voice is full of life.
She dances as her body moves with grace.
She poses like a model as her movement
Spreads like a sculpture of art.

She is a wandering flower.
She moves as the wind
Blows on a warm, sunny
Spring day.
She changes different seasons
Every time the climate changes.
She moves across the field
Like a beautiful dancer,
Dancing in the distance sunset.

She is the morning sunrise.
She is the evening sky.
She is the middle of the night
As the stars
Reach out to talk to her.
She is like a silent
Dancer with ballerina shoes,
Tiptoeing around with
No tone of emotion.
She dances through the body.

She is a sunflower with a beautiful smile,
Feeling so happy inside with a lot of pride.
Let's capture a photo of this sunflower beauty.
She will take you on a journey.
Look at her dancing, teaching us a lesson.
She is a beautiful sunflower.

Shavonda Robinson

The Life of a Red Rose

Red roses, come find me.
Red roses fall over the sea
Coming into its own.
Red roses have a lively voice.
Teardrops seem to pour into a mystified fall.
I see red roses on the ground.
For someone, love is in red roses.

I step into the name of roses.
I am floating on a boat in the ocean.
I hear thunder roaring in the background.
Oh, it's rolling clouds
Grab onto the joy.
Red roses, come find me.
Red roses, I will follow you into ecstasy
Until you die.

Lay you in red satin,
Float you down the river,
When I begin to bury you in one peace.
If you die again so young,
Red roses fall down in fantasy,
Chase you like a remedy.
Red roses play an actor in September.

Red roses pour out traces of blood,
Red roses in a vase on the table by the window,
Then I start to remember all the unique things
Of a red rose who has brought new birth of life.
I held two red roses in my hand
On a Ferris wheel.
It symbolizes the love I have for the
Two most important people in my life.
The children I have born.
Come on, follow me, red roses;
Let's lift up sunlight in our lives.

Piano Man

Thoughts race across the sky.
Where will you land, piano man?
Teach me how to say
Your name in French.
Give yourself an applause.
Give me that feeling once again;
Thoughts reminisce like a love song.

Waterdrops flow out of the gate.
Inseparable glances will lead the way.
Piano man, take it away.
Music fills up the room,
Thoughts race across the sky,
Painting all over our goodbyes.

Express yourself to me.
Where will you stand,
Way of the world?
Saying hello to me,
Music notes became louder and louder,
Drowning thoughts land into the bay.
Ignited flights at night
Shine over the sea.
Baby boy, dream on,
Piano man will begin the show.

Don't ignore the music.
Give yourself an applause.
Make tomorrow so beautiful.
Where will you stand,
How will you land,
By a plane or a ship?
Holding on feels like forever,
Kiss for a kiss,
Cheek to cheek,
Time is coming on.
Piano man loves to create music.

Twirling my emotions upside down,
Waiting by the water fountains;
Here you are, lover,
But I still wonder
In the back of my mind,
When will you take off tonight?
Where will you land?
Your wishes are my command.

Praise Thy Glory

Praise thy lord,
Praise thy lord,
Praise his name,
Praise his name.
Here I rise above all complicated things.
You set me free,
Lord, sent me a message from heaven.
I received it from one of your angels,
Telling me to stay strong
No matter what.

We all rise to fall.
Wake up, this is his last call.
Flying angels flowing out of heaven
To greet me in his honor of acceptance.
Here is a gift of patience
Through all the stormy dazes
That tried to rock my faith,
Believing in you.

Now the weather is bright and sunny.
Oh, Lord, you are my best friend.
I know I can call on you
Whenever I need you.

I give you praise, Lord,
I give you praise, Lord.
You brought me back
From anything that came my way
When I felt the most helpless
In my life.

I just want to say thank you,
My Lord and Savior, for being
My dearest friend.
You showed me the way to your heart.
You showed me how
I should please you;
Not take your word for granted.
Your way is the only path
To an everlasting life in happiness.

Glowing Wings

I am a dancer with glowing wings.
Music lights up the stage.
Touch me, tease me,
Do you know what I mean;
Time creates a piece of reality?

I sang out loud to the sound,
Saying ooh la la la la to the beat.
Take a seat, I spin around,
My feet are off the ground.
I am a dancer with glowing wings.
I move to my own beat.

I dance in the dark,
Ripping my clothes off,
Showing how bright my colors as a dancer
Really are.
Glow crazy, glow crazy,
Confessions, I am a dancer with glowing wings.
Come on, come on,
Put your body up against mine
In the dark,
Where no one can see our colorful secrets.

I am a dancer with glowing wings,
I glide right through you,
Like water flowing down the stream.
I dance as the music
Becomes louder and louder.
I feel so free spirited
When I am dancing in the dark all alone.
I know when you are thinking of me;
The music has a sexy tone.

Thoughts on a Platform

Thoughts soaked the paper
When I touch it with my mind.
Staring at these words,
The depth of meaning on a platform
Became a joke.

Translating verbal nonsense language
Soon became deaf
When it comes to my own voice.
Private thoughts build their own hibernation,
Tell me quiet thoughts,
Are you still racing for definitions?

I can't hear those words,
I can't hear those words
Falling onto my paper
Like raindrops.

Mature thoughts pollute my mind
When I am high off inspiration.

Thoughts immerse themselves in victory.
I am an innovator in this new age,
Never going out of style,
Twenty-first century poet
Since the beginning of time.
Shower me with thoughts of blank stares.
The words are silent.
I emerge from a stubborn words disorder
On top of the platform.
Thoughts drop like wet
Cold raindrops onto the surface.

There goes thoughts racing around
Like a wild circus.

My words are soundless actions.
Raindrops wet the pages.
Liquid motions continue to build no notions
As the poet's voice gets lower and lower.
I cannot hear myself speak or think out loud.
A word is just a word only on paper as they jump
Out at me.

Shavonda Robinson

Flower Despair Song

Drip drop, the paint splatters on the floor.
The flower paints a picture of a sad reality.
It blossoms into the air;
It bleeds out poisonous seeds.

Traces of blood affect the flower
I picked from the bush.
Gave it to Lorene and Sanaya.
They held it in their hands so tightly.
I caught the jealous disease;
Suffocation misleads me.

The flower paints out
So many sad moods.
What a believable sight to see
The blood leaked on my hands.
I sang out song cries from my heart
As Lorene and Sanaya
Gently stroked me with comfort.
The flower creates undefined paintings
Of sad faces.
She is slowly losing her grip on life;
I won't let her go.

Contaminated blood was left
All over the house.
The flower's tears are endless to all fears,
Stricken with HIV Virus.
We all act normal surrounding her with love
In this cold world.

I can see the flower mania,
Struggling to survive this life.
Stolen pride catches the flower
As it continues to die
One day at a time.
Puddles of tears began to fall
From the flower mania eyes.
Lorene and Sanaya
Skip along down the sidewalk,
Waiting for a signal.
The flower still cries.
No one wants to follow.
Flower mania's last days
Strive to be an empty, empty
Plea for a song cry.
As the flowers bleed out
Poisonous seeds once again,
Flower mania just took her last breath yesterday
And died instantly.

Turquoise Rain

She blows in the wind;
Her color is turquoise.
Awakened raindrops knock on her window.
His hands touch her in a guilty way,
She begins to say her soul ran away
With the turquoise rain.

Blue and white diamonds on the floor,
She found a piece of her in a hopeless place.
She wrote her name on the walls;
She has completely gone insane.

The color of emotions come alive;
A lifeless feeling.
Blue and white diamonds hail little Mary.
He started a rebel terrorizing her innocence
Of doubt.
She refuses to be his sinner.
Red flames burn up his hands.
Turquoise rain spreads out emotional rings.

She pounds and stamps on the floor.
No one is listening to her.
She spins in a dizzy
Spell of coldness.
She runs all the way up the long hill
And falls over the cliff into the deep water
Of the ocean.
Now she has drowned.
She makes no more sounds.
Turquoise rain pours out sorrowful memories.
Sad story carries on forever as it glows
Into the turquoise rain.

Little Mary has her spirits haunting
Over the old house.
As he struggles to deal with
Her little spirit coming to haunt him
In regret.
Turquoise rain spreads its emotion all over.
Her soul is lost on hollow ground.

Shavonda Robinson

The Walls of Poetry

Let me tear down
The walls of old poetry.
Let me build up
The walls of new poetry.
Let me drive in my own lane.
No, I am not insane.
I live to create a genre
Called the new poetry.

Poetic magic rings out loud;
Makes the nation
Open up their eyes
And come alive.
The walls of poetry
Are gonna rise up.
The ladder to fame,
Let me tear down.
The walls of old poetry
Rebuild the new version
For the future ideal.

I have painted all sorts of definitions
Not to be divided by the old way.
Let's experience the new chapter
Of poetry;
No rules to follow.
Let me tear down
The walls of old poetry,
Make waves across the sky,
Showing love for the new poetry
I have created for the world.

Let the new poetry
Follow the light.
Let me tear down
Those old poetry walls.
Poetry is alive again.
I reinvented it; old poetry is no more,
Making room for future poetry.
New ways to follow,
Mainstream will grab on and
Not let go.

Let me build up
The walls of new poetry;
Tear down the walls of old poetry.
Remember, poetry is alive again;
I reinvented it.
So when you write it,
Think of me
Whenever you see poetry alive.
Poetry is engrained in my veins.

Pen Thoughts

Pen is in motion,
Here comes a notion,
Setting a stage in front of us,
My hand begin to scribble.
Thoughts spark up new ideas,
But I refuse to feel neglected.
Words bear their souls to me
In a secret position
No one can know.
Secrets pitch a ball into the air;
Whoa! Look at it go.

Words became exploited.
I started to feel dirty.
I play with creativity until
It turned into inspiration.
Pen thoughts, pen thoughts
Backfired in a explosion.
Shake the ideas out,
Depth comes walking onto the page.

Takes on life adventures,
Pen thoughts create a home
For those aspiring minds.
We engage in excitement.
It's all about stirring the imagination.
The page is a friendly environment
For all creations to arise into something special.

Pen thoughts penetrate into
A motion of circles.
We follow skills of showmanship,
Giving it a touch of creativity.
Pen thoughts come to life
In a whole new way.

Pen thoughts, pen thoughts
Pen thoughts, pen thoughts.

Freestyle Inspiration

The poet in me
Skips to the beat.
I dance on speakers.
The music uplifts me.
Inspirations circle around me.
We are young forever,
Still holding onto a false mentally.
Leftover love,
I lost my appetite.

Rational changes flow beyond
Creative juices.
I began to lose control.
The poet in me begins to speak.
The words keep on repeating themselves.
Freestyle dancers perform as
The music continues to play on,

The heart of a poet sings
Songs.

We are young forever.
We are young tonight.
Let's all play dress-up
Like curious kids do
And run around with no worries.
I can be a queen too,
Be classy like old folks do.
The poet in me needs rescuing,
To bring out the truth of beauty in you.

Poetic flows come from the music.
Everything amuses us,
Dancing on tables pretending
We are teenagers.
Speakers blow sky high.
Freestyle inspirations come out of the heart.
The poet in me
Begins to speak out loud,
Says to you,
"Don't disturb our fun tonight.
Feelings begin to disappear,
Peeling off layers.
We are young,
Or maybe I just love to have fun."

Shavonda Robinson

Coloring God's Picture

I followed God's voice
Somewhere over the rainbow.
I got lost on the path.
I used dark-colored crayons,
But he never liked dark colors
On the canvas,
So I used bright colors to make
The picture more beautiful and realistic.
I embraced God's sense of style
When it comes to his artistic personality.

I followed God's voice of thought.
Somehow, I got trampled on by ideas.
Somewhere, somehow,
I still hear him calling out for me,
God's message to me.
He is a messenger,
He creates many masterpieces,
So I made him a creation.
I followed God's ministry.
He led me into his path
Of wisdom.

I used all his favorite colors
In the crayon box.
God's teardrops I found
Soaked on my sleeve.
He said to me,
This is the most beautiful picture
He has ever seen.
I colored a picture of judgement day.

He holds out his hands,
Saying to me,
Your colors have changed his creative ways.
You are made to entertain,
For the love of colors on a canvas.

Oh, Sadie, Thoughts

Who painted the sky blue?
So sky away my thoughts of you,
My God shows you his true mood,
Twinkling stars come at you.
As time flies above me,
Oh, Sadie cries for you.

My God took a paintbrush,
Colored the heavenly skies so blue.
Hopeless dreams float on a cloud,
Just like God made you and me.
My God, I am telling you why
I will not follow the tainted crowd.

So sky away another day of beautiful things.
Oh Sadie, oh Sadie, oh Sadie,
Time is coming toward you.
So run away with my love,
Dear Mr. Jesus.
I swear I want you to see how curiosity
Has struck me blind,
But still you always will be a friend of mine.

Dear God, I would love to be
Your precious queen.
I belong to your fruitful garden
Doing all the righteous things.
My God, I can see you painting
The world in all colors.

Who painted the sky blue?
My precious God is the creator of all things.
Oh, Sadie, oh Sadie, oh Sadie,
Did you hear what I said?
My God painted the sky blue.

Time flies above me,
Do you see what I see,
Teardrops and rainbows
Shine in the sky above me?
Let's capture the moment
As I wish for all beautiful things,
I will promise to save you from tomorrow.

Oh, Sadie, take my hand;
Runaway with me now.
Oh, Sadie, you still ask me
Who painted the sky blue?
Just like he made you and me,
Two different human beings,
Believing in unique things.

Black Sparrow Sorrow

The red rose began to rise,
His eyes on a black sparrow are lost forever.
He transforms into a lifeless spirit,
He is sacred and lonely;
Flies off the edge into a hidden mystery.

Black sparrow leaps through the air,
His words full of despair.
Waterdrops filled the sky
One last time.
Black sparrow finds his spoken words,
Heartbreak is a mistake
As he flies away.

The black sparrow begins to mature.
I see its true beauty,
From a seed to a bloom flower,
Inside of his emotions carry
A lot of power.

Black sparrow carries it as
His powerful words on a row.

High flying black sparrow,
Soaring over his heartfelt emotions.
Black sparrow drops sorrow
Into the ocean water.

Black sparrow on a row;
He hears musical notes.
Emotions fall from his eyes.
Black sparrow continues to cry.
He hides secrets from the world's eye.
Look on the inside.
He is a lonely, sad bird
Without a home.

Through his eyes,
Happiness never has been
A part of his world.
Black sparrow flies away
In the sky.
No one wonders where
He came from.

All I know is we saw
Black sparrow carrying a red rose
In his mouth.
Sitting on a row,
Black sparrow's spoken words were declined
As he flew to find a new home.

Shavonda Robinson

Inspirational Kind of Woman

I am an inspirational kind of woman.
I have no wings to fly.
I spread beauty across the world,
My personality comes alive,
My imagination is full of life,
I stay in grace.
My flair and confidence never goes out of style,
But I don't let the hard times
Bring me down.

My knowledge will always age.
True beauty is a reflection of you.
I live for inspiring things.
I am a strong, beautiful, confident woman;
No one can take that glory away,
I wear the crown of these inspiring words
On my head.

I am an inspiration kind of woman.

I stand strong with pride,
I feel so beautiful and
I accept myself for who I am.
Every old wound
I had in the past
Has healed up inside;
I believe in me.

I found my own inner peace,
No longer feeling bittersweet,
I am the best me
I can be.
I know who I am inside.
My identity screams out
So much pride.

I am an inspirational kind of woman.

I live by love,
I live for eternity,
I feel on top of the world,
I am my own kinda girl,
Creating my own story.

I am an inspirational kind of woman.

The world is full of opportunities
For everyone.
I live by these inspiring words-
Be yourself and the rest
Of things in life
Will fall into place.

Listen to me.
Silence at this moment-
We as inspirational women
Can do anything we want.
The world belongs to no one
But God.
Listen to the message;
These are the words
Of an inspiring woman.

Written Dedication

I hope I can dance with you in the sky,
Write our memories for you and me.
Hey, God, I am talking to you.
Last night you came to me,
In a realistic dream and said,
"Wake up, girl, follow your dreams."

God is my witness,
I feel the holy ghost
Coming out of me.
You continued to say,
"I gave you a poetic voice
To express across the world."

Floating on poetry bites,
God sang me a song.
He told me to spread
My messages as it flies up to heaven.
Showcase my colorful wings,
I shine bright in my own light,
Oh, God! My thoughts can fly so high.
When I write, I feel so alive.

Shavonda Robinson

There's no caging my pride.
Oh, God! I am telling you why,
For the love of spoken words
Never dies in my eyes.
I feel the fire.
I hope you and I can dance in the sky.

My God, as the letters fall from heaven,
God, please write me another message.
I will dance like a star in your heart.
I can use a crayon and color a picture
So bright in our imaginations.
We belong together.

I love the riddles of my rhythm lyrics.
Runs through my body
Like a electric shock.
Please show me your powers
At least you can set me free.
Speak to me,
I am down on my knees
Praying to thee.

In the name of God,
I give thanks to bringing colorful
Words on a platform.

We all can adore.
Open the doors,
Look at me,
I got a gift to share with you and others.

Just like the flurry feathers on a bird,
They flock together.
Poems flew up to heaven
As I dance in the sky with you
For the last time.

What a beautiful adventure.
I can't deny God spoke to me
As he danced across the sky.
He waved to me goodbye,
He blew a kiss at me,
When I looked up at God
Floating on by.

I knew deep down inside,
It was time for me to show the world
What I got.
Pour magical sprinkles on me.
Look as they begin to twinkle,
Because I am a shining star.

Shavonda Robinson

Colorful Melody

You turned into a butterfly.
Spread your wings, it's time to fly.
Colors grew brighter as the sun smiled
With laughter,
The further you go away.
So many colors on a butterfly,
You start to change.
The phrases of your reflection
Faded away with a distant, beautiful melody.

You see the butterflies
Making nature into its own work
Of art.
Decorating the flowers in May
For a scene,
Reaching beyond human beings'
Capacity to seek beauty.
The picture of bright colors
Sparkling gleam in the air.

The butterflies fly away so fast;
When you try to reach them,
You can't grab on.
Losing hope on the butterflies,
Maybe one day you will return home
To see all those old butterflies
Flying in the sky,
Enjoying old memories,
Gripping onto reality.
Colorful melody plays on
As they flutter on into happiness.

Spinning Webs to an Imagination

She is a genius and imaginative woman,
Creating the most amazing webs of letters
Across the city.
Hanging from the words of imagery city,
Glistening in the sunray eyes to disobey.
Together we can make spinning webs like a maze,
Taking on glittery words who paint the city.

She moves so quickly, acting so suspicious,
Spinning webs like a trick of trades up
Her sleeve,
Writing the letters of her name in the web
So everyone can see her talent
Was so amazing.
Eventually, she will reach fame.

She is a rising star wordsmith woman.
Climbing in her web,
Ready to conquer the world,
When sparkles of colors strike out
By fountain of landscapes.

She is best known for
Creating webs of words so beautifully.
Swinging high in the sky,
She colours up her webs,
So she can keep an eye
On her wild imagination.
She is magical to see.
She has powers to create flowing
Designs,
Spinning webs into the rhymes and letters,
A constant of a vowel
Reaches to a loud sound.

Imaginative woman in her own world
Takes on a mission to create
Webs of words as she climbs
The height of her imagination.
She sets out to save the world.

This is her vision.
She creates a web of artistry
As she spins and twists
Into her own creations.

Riddle Man

There's a man with riddles,
He has a poetic flair.
Undress me by your words,
I will let down my hair.
You sparkle me so poetically,
Give me all of your creative words.
I wanna fall in love with your poetry.

I am in a creative mood.
Come here and sit down;
Let's write some rhymes together.
I see the beauty in you.
Your words can't defined who you are.

You are a wordsmith kinda guy.
People stand up to notice,
Your words are beautifully arranged
From your lips.
Take off my clothes, magical man,
Your hands are filled with lyrics.
Let me dive into your poems.
Take me home with you.

Can you write riddles into my soul?
You are my poetic soul,
You are my riddle man with
A poetic soul sings.
Oh, lyrical man, oh, lyrical man,
Your poetry is so beautiful to me.

Shavonda Robinson

Poems of the World

Hello again!
These are the poems
Of the world.
You as a viewer,
You as a believer.
Poems of the world
Come alive.
They strive to live on
For eternity.

You as a listener,
Poems, do you feel
An inspiring mood
Coming through you?
Treasury is brought to me
By the gift of life.
God gave me his blessings.
Thank you, my God.
So I write to entertain
The world.
These are the poems
Of the world.
Beauty is like reality.
Thoughts are the power
Of written words.

Poems speak so loudly.
The world sees you;
Hello, world! Hello, you!
The people scream and shout,
Hooray! Hooray!
The poems showcase themselves
Across the world.
Look at the momentum value.
We see poetry is the truth.

These are the poems
Of the world.
Speaking loud and clear,
This is our time.
We command your attention,
Written words,
We carry a deep talkative soul.

Hello, world! Hello, you!
These are the poems
Of the world.
Timeless means historic artistry.
The world knows it.
The poems carry their own voice.
The poems carry a rich tone.
The world appreciates you.
Hello, world!
These are the poems
Of the world.

Watercolors Expression

This is my expression.
I create a landscape of colors.
I can paint you
A vision of Jesus
Walking on water.
He created the deep, blue sea.
He speaks to me.
Oh, life is but a dream.

Wake up, my dear.
Can't you see
Mr. Jesus looking at me?
We both agree,
The time has come
Not to be blind.
Open your eyes;
Jesus is once again alive.
This is my expression.
I create a landscape of colors
On the board.
Jesus' face is here to embrace.

This is our land.
Jesus walks on the sea.
Jesus speaks to all of the world.
I show Jesus my pastels
As I paint a vision of what I see.
Jesus reaches out to me.
I reach out to him.
Hello, again!

Do you see Jesus?
This is an unbelievable moment,
Showing everybody love.
Listen to him! Listen to him!
As he makes a crucial speech.
Jesus walks through the sea.

This is my expression.
We were made from dust.
To dust we shall return.
Watercolors all over the world,
Jesus walks through the sea
Speaking to all of thee.
This is my expression.
Mr. Jesus.
Yes, I see you.
Hold on, take me with you.
Where are you going?
This is our land of watercolors
From your mighty powers.

Riding Colors

Take a walk into my thoughts.
Visualize everything I see within me.
The world is full of colors and ideas.
Ride a wave into my finding imagination.
There is a bright woman somewhere locked
Inside me
Who has a creative mind.
Going off into wonderland,
Take a walk into my ideas;
The place I've built is made out of someone's imagination.
Take a look at its own beauty,
The piece of color's capturement is a timeless memory.
I wonder about a lot of things.
This is a place for all colors to survive
In the depth of an individual.
Dive into a journey of ideas.
We all want a colorful life
Look all around; colors and ideas
Are everywhere.

Fallen Galaxy

I will wait for this day
To see you again.
Cherishing time away from you,
I see everything in a different light.

Sailing through life without you
Would be obscure to my faithful heart.
Today we celebrate your birthday;
I emphasis the signs of life celebrations.

I count the candles on the cake.
I wish you were here with me.
Fantasy awaits my aspiring imagination.
When I dream upon you,
Memories hold wishes near your heart.

Fallen galaxies spin around you.
Goodbyes will send you
A kiss to the sky
As we count down the days
When I see your face.

Eccentric Messages

Sometimes, I cry.
Sometimes, I wonder.
Laughter runs beyond,
A thunder we are in vain,
But somehow his messages go insane.

Listen to my heartbeat.
God is crying.
His teardrops pour outside the window.
No one is a re-sender of lost messages.

Time ages on forever.
We are caged in a corrupted zone.
Then, I ask myself,
Is it lonely at the top
Being a unique individual
Chosen for dedication?

We are leaders.
We are followers.
Sometimes, I grasp for eccentric rhymes,
I hear echoes of God's voice,
I am a soldier with hardcore war scars
Living behind bars in my own prison.

Beautiful Blues

She was a hidden vision,
All alone in her room.
She plays the flute so beautifully;
It whistles to the sound of praise.
She sings through the flute of despair.
One day she got the courage
To perform on stage,
Let the whole world hear her voice.
When she plays the flute, her songs began
To fall.

She plays the flute as the purple haze
Filled her heart moods.
The theme of her song
Plays along, sounding so peacefully.
She was an invisible, shy, insecure girl.
Once upon a time, girls would tease her for
Being an outcast.
No one knew
She was a beautiful flute player
Who could relate to the blues
She felt inside her soul.

She plays the flute
All alone in her room,
Writing songs on her instrument.
She's an amazing talent ready to be discovered.
The sounds of her
Playing the flute travel through the air.

Her songs will remind you
Of some beautiful poetry.
As she plays the flute,
There was a song about her
Father committing suicide
When she was just two years old.
She captured so many hearts,
In the crowd with a beautiful song.
It was so heartfelt and powerful,
No one knew she was a beautiful flute player.

Glowing Truth

Trains of thought
Rising up like a thick, hazy vapor
Appearing in the air.
I swear the hand I was dealt,
I could never tell.
Personal issues recording its way of a difficult
Situation to understand.

Issues we face today
Glows truth in a solid place.
Life's shackles can't erase pleading memories
Riding like a fast lane
Train on a track shifting out of control.
Flashing problems remain like shifting time away
As we stand up and say,
Our issues fall down
Like mist from the air.

Shavonda Robinson

Honey dew in the morning,
We all got the news,
We know the truth.
Issues place themselves
On the front page of our lives.
We all got problems
To solve in our lives.
Or do we have time to care for all?
We should be leaders and helpers
To each other in this world.

Problems develop out of nowhere.
We all can tell.
We can feel it in the air.
Glowing truth arrives in our lives,
Everyday.
We walk over it with no shame.
Let's play the game.
Fairly you get a turn,
I get a turn.
I am the champion,
You are the challenger
To your own glowing truth.

Surface of Bubbles

The bubbles foam into a surface,
Only showing its face.
When it is a clear substance to a realistic eye,
So many textures have developed into its own persona.
Changing bubbles float all over the place.
You can catch them, but you must be quick in action.

The bubbles of life have taken their own course
To excel in a greater living,
A platform if bubbles must have a starter to blow
All over to create a scene.

We live as bubbles have become in a stuck mode.
Troubling times follow our bubbles and translate
As we see the light.
Clear bubbles, we can see right through you
Like a piece of plastic.
Floating bubbles all around you,
One by one to pop them in your hands.
Every bubble has its own legend.

We as individuals seeking our purpose,
Blowing bubbles rise in the air.
Whether small, medium, or big,
Poor, middle class, and rich,
We come as our own kind
In a row following a line,
Bubbles are blown out everywhere.

We look out to see
Who are the bubbles of our reality.
We all are bubbles
Floating around on the scene.

Bubbles flow toward me.
This is who I see.
You are a storytelling rumor spreading
Like a trend of fashion.
Bubbles live for a profound reason of beauty.
Again, we are bubbles,
Sprouting up like the wonders of surprises.
Beyond opinions of all bubbles rotate, one in a billion,
And multiplying on this curious earth.

Circulation of Shapes

Making circles,
Making triangles,
Making squares,
Making ovals,
Making rectangles, transforming into spirals,
Figures on the page.

The characters of shapes
Gives you artistic inspiration.
Here are the lives of shapes,
Coloring on the pages.
Reshaping the contours of our landscapes,
Circulation drives through a colorful
Change in our literary art backgrounds.

Shapes give incredible shine
To different images.
Making shapes becomes a standpoint
of visional eyes,
Decorations of shapes attaching onto life figures.

Here's the page with shapes
You can see with your own eyes.
Are you really surprised
Making shapes becomes a part of our lives?
Striving to create a photographic vision
Of colorful shapes,
In all powerful turns
Forming amazing works.
Here we see the aspirations and compliments
Of moving shapes on blank pages
As we sit there and stare at the page
Taking on its own life.

Flying Actions

Ooh! Actions, I like your style,
So free, so wild.
Liberate me from wondering off.
Actions scream out loud,
Flying through the air,
Soaring like an airplane,
Actions spell out thy name.

Traces of actions,
Painting a scene,
Jumping over it like a trampoline,
Describing actions became an actor.
Taste the consequences based
On every decision.
Thriving to suffer, actions unfold to deliver.

Falling down becomes an action.
Would you please tell the child quit frowning,
There's no clowning around?
Actions have wings to fly over the world,
Spreading actions like fairy dust.

Ooh! Actions, I like your style,
So free, so wild.
Liberate actions to be released.
Actions became the greatest flyer
I've ever seen.

Writing Rainbows

Writing on a rainbow,
Here I am reading a book.
I turn the page,
Here is the story of my life.
I finish up the chapters,
My life is mapped out in stages.

If fifty thousand people read me,
Why won't you see me?
How could this book relate to you?
Just remember, it all started
When I was writing on a rainbow.

I look like a ordinary girl
Writing her thoughts out, here I am,
Reading a book in the park,
Sitting on a bench,
This is me.
Do you remember me?
Quiet girl, bright girl,
Just like you.

No superstars are born today.
Writing on a rainbow,
Imagination takes me to a place
Where I can be free to roam.
Words of the century kinda girl,
Here I am, open up a book,
You will find me.
Just stare at the pages,
Immerse yourself in the rainbow.

Still I began to feel
Like walking on stone,
Thought for thought.
Just remember, I was the girl
Writing on the rainbow.
Here I am,
Quiet girl, bright girl,
This is me.

In this moment,
Why is everyone staring at me?
Writing on a rainbow
In a bright place,
I want you to read me.
Silence drives the engine of pride.

I began to break down
The words inside of me.
Writing on a rainbow,
Here I am.
Will you remember me?
Quiet girl, bright girl,
Read a passage in the park.
Words of the century
Splashing colors like crazy,
You will have a bright life
Writing rainbows.

Thundering Away

The sun is chasing
The clouds away.
Keep on singing,
Keep on singing,
Thundering, Thundering;
You are so afraid to cry
This way?
Teardrops fall to embrace
Right there in your hands.
The clouds got away.
Keep on thundering,
Keep on thundering;
Say hey to yesterday.

I saw you rolling, rolling, rolling.
The clouds seem to meet.
Teardrops thunder here in grace.
Let her see you cry.
Keep on wondering,
Keep on wondering;
Where have you been?
The clouds are drops
Away from sunshine,
Maybe another day?

The sun is chasing
The clouds away,
Thundering away,
Thundering away,
The skies turn grey.

Thoughts hanging around,
Sounds call out to the sky.
Keep on thundering,
Keep on thundering,
Where do teardrops begin to fall?
Being too blind to see reality,
Lifeless clouds rolling by.
Keep on singing,
Keep on singing,
Thoughts smile at glory.
I see you chasing the sun;
I see you chasing the clouds
As they roll on by.

Sad man sings a riddle faraway.
Can you hear it,
Lonely teardrops,
Thundering up a scattered storm?
Thundering away,
Thundering away,
Why are you so afraid to cry;
I am wondering will you ever change?

Why is the thundering as loud
The sky moves away tonight?
The cloud's spoken languages
Cry all day.
Thundering away,
Thundering away,
In the clouds go rolling by.
Keep on thundering,
Keep on thundering,
I am left wondering,
Why would you just get on
With crying?
The sky is crying out teardrops
For you.

The clouds are chasing
Our sun away.
Here is a beautiful change today.
I see you chasing teardrops.
Here goes you smiling at the sun.
Keep on thundering,
Keep on thundering.
Why don't you cry out loud?

Awaken Beginnings

The shadow of tomorrow
Awakens new beginnings.
Morning dew on my pane,
Somehow I went away with the wind.
Deep thoughts arise again,
Colorful images surround our quest.
Sequence stories become an
Open dedicated friend.
Send a kiss to a faithful man,
Saying hello again.
There is a halo in your presence.
Falling notions pose like
A sweet potion stand in glory.
Behold, hail Mary before me.
The shadows of tomorrow
Awaken new beginnings.

Morning dew on my window pane,
Cold raindrops pour from the dark sky,
Here I am waiting for the moment
For us to live forever.

Time is now, time is now,
The shadows of tomorrow have arrived.
Awaken new beginnings,
Open your eyes.

Suffocating Emotions

There is a feeling of hopelessness in emotions
Where the skies are blue,
Take me away.
Suffocating, there is no room
For pouring emotions,
Just a misunderstood girl
Who is hard as a shell.
Time will eventually tell,
Where do the melodies
Begin to fall.
There is a hopeless place
For emotions
That is clear to see.
Red roses, blue tulips
Begin to talk to me.

My song is an old tune.
Go ahead and play the violin,
My dear.
Where the skies are blue
Hanging emotions turn misty blue.
Sometimes, my eyes go blind,
Yet, my soul is still crying,
Waiting for an empty explanation.
This is a destination
Where the skies are blue.
A hopeless void comes over me.
Can't wait one minute more
On our own glory.
Take me away to a faraway land,
Sand in between my feet,
I walk on imaginable ground.
Boom! There is no sound.
Dragging emotions start to drown,
Build a dungeon downtown
Where the skies are blue.

Runaway Burdens

My thoughts have ran away,
Have vanished from sight.
My voice has lost its place,
My thoughts carry an empty burden.
These words are mine,
Got emptied into the trash.
In a wandering state of mind
I would love to decline.
My voice has been caged today,
But I still pray to you
One last time.

Runaway words, there's no pride for you
To hide in the dark.
There is a fascinating story out there
Waiting on you.
My voice, my words
Have ran away from me.
Please, my voice I am screaming,
Come back to me.

I need you now,
My thoughts have vanished from sight.
It is a mysterious case.
Ain't got nothing on my mind,
My words stand still in silence.
This is how I feel
In an empty, deaf-toned
State of mind.
These words of mine,
My voice is slowly fading away
Out of sight.

Dream of Wisdom

High flying above on my thoughts,
I run across the sea to a field of ideas,
To a creation of wishful thinking out loud,
My reflection paints a dream.
Look into a deep view of yourself.
Who do you see a powerful theme
In a range of different colors?
I will fly on a plane, waiting for you,
I rise on a sparkling dream of life,
Starring the road to wisdom.

The creation to our reality,
Picture me as a painted portrait.
Draw a masterpiece behind a formality;
Hey, pure vision take me on a vision.

Writing on a concrete ground,
I found depth inside,
A lonely dark place,
No one is to blame.
Welcome to my life's vision.
I see what we have become,
All invisible to each one's eyes.

Thy Paintbrush to Abstracting Images

Here is my life,
I call my own,
Beginning to the end.
A storyline is a narration
Verse to the world.
My voice will be heard once again,
Only if we touch the golden eternity
Of things.
Weird beauty floats on by in the mind;
A wise girl writes her life on by.
Tell me why
Falling lies from the sky
Appear tonight?
Collides beside our infinity,
An opening lyrical spirit
To the wizard queen.

Here is my strength
Producing into brave hearts,
Written from a concrete feeling.
You behold,
From a born again wise girl,
Nobody knows the true meaning of you.

When you become the dream
Of wisdom,
Come find me and tell me
What's going on?
Here, come fly on a wishful plane
With me,
As we look into a dream of you,
Still I will be waiting on you.

Shavonda Robinson

A Rose to Mama

She is standing there.
Hello, mama!
I give you this beautiful rose.
Hold out your hands to me.
I will set you free.
You gave me the gift of love.
Your love for me soars so high.

Here, I present you with these
Lovely thoughts.
No sharp thorns are attached
When I think of you.
You are such a beautiful woman
With a freely soul.
Come here to me, mama.
Spread your wings.
Fly away in the sky.

Mama, look at the sea.
It brought you back to me.
Rising like a red rose,
You helped me grow
From a seed to a mature flower.

Thy Paintbrush to Abstracting Images

I can see you still holding on.
Mama dearest, you gave me
The gift of life.

I owe it all to you.
You are the kind of woman
I thrive to be.
But there is no comparison to you.
God sent you to me on his wings.
You hold a special place in my heart.

A beautiful angel flies over me.
I believe it is you.
You carried me.
I owe you this beautiful rose.
She is standing there.
Hello, mama!
Roses fall down on you
Like raindrops.

I will set you free at last.
You gave me the gift of life.
I will always hold you
Close to my heart.
As roses come to life,
Oh, mama, you are a precious gift
In my life.
Your love stands for a symbol
Of red roses
That no one can replace.
This is for you, mama.
You are my beautiful red rose.

This poem is dedicated to my beautiful mother.

Farewell, My Wings

I can see beneath your beautiful wings.
It used to be flying beside you.
I am floating across the river,
Open stream alone now.
When did the stars become sparky silver.
Yes, I got the farewell note
You left behind.
You are going somewhere away from here.
Can I follow you?
I just want to be where you are.
My emotions are broken up in pieces.

I said farewell to my favorite stars
As I wished for you in the sky.
I miss you dreadfully.
I blow a kiss into the air.
A hundred days have passed on by;
You are living a new life.
Farewell, my love.
Farewell, my friend.
Is this where it ends?
I understand you had to go
Where you can be free.
I gotta be a big girl now
And spread my wings, too.

Farewell, my love.
Farewell, my friend.
Take me with you.
My heart beats slower by day.
If you got time,
I wanna tell you
What's on my mind,
But this will only be
Words passing by you.
Really, my thoughts never knew you.
Can we go to a land called far away?

You are going somewhere to
Free yourself.
I hope that you are happy
Sailing across the world.
Farewell, my love.
Farewell, my friend.
This is where we will end.

Poetic Divas

My thoughts are absent for tomorrow,
So I write this in your honor.
Free verse is a base
For flirting with words.
Show me your wordplay.
Can I come out to play?
Look at them ideas
Dancing on the table.

I dare to become a dazzling jewel
In your eyes,
Twirling your jet black locks
With your fingertips,
Reinventing our funhouse.
Words became our playground,
Super hyper woman, oh! That's my luck
Hopping onto the page.
Poetry helps define its place.
We can create whatever.
It's nobody's business but
The creator itself.

My thoughts are absent for tomorrow.
Today I feel like painting
The world different colors.
This is a funhouse
Only for creative souls.
Everyone is not welcome,
So poetry starts to ignore.

I became a poetic diva.
Believe me, I know
How it feels to be on the other
End of the receiver.
Please, this will never be me
For too long.
Perhaps, I am weird.
Oh well, take notice.
Most weirdos are some kind of geniuses.
Perhaps I look for weird things to take place.

Laughter Teardrops

Are you a tear of the cloud's conversation?
If so, I feel raindrops bringing itself back to life.
Laughter began to strike its presence,
Raising a prayers mission.
I awaken to the sound of thunder
Calling on thee.

Say my name.
Bring me blue tulips
If you can.
As we lay awakened
In tomorrow's dreamland,
There's no identity in truth.
Do you see the passion in our views?

As we bow,
I simply admire beauty
As I look around.
Are you a tear of the clouds conversation,
Above, soaring slowly?
I see raindrops smiling
Back at me.
If so, I feel liberated,
Sending away someone's
Hopes and dreams.

Hello, moving clouds.
Can I talk to you?
We continue to write a notion
Of happiness together.
Are you a tear of the cloud's conversation?
If so, I feel
Like God has given me
A place called freedom.

Beyond our wishes,
I envision raindrops dripping on my head
As I contemplate my next thoughts.
Are you a tear of the cloud's conversation?
Envision all things to live in eternity
On moving trials.

I forgot we live for his voice.
Are you a tear of the cloud's conversation?
Infinity clouds go spinning around,
Dropping raindrops all over town.
I see written thoughts
Spreading apart too far.
We live for this hour.
Are you a tear of the cloud's conversation?
As I look around,
I see your beauty.

About the Author

Shavonda Robinson is an accomplished writer whose credits include being published in a few anthologies and magazines. She also is the founder of "Create Something for the Future", an online poetry magazine for upcoming poets and writers. She has won a few poetry awards for being most creative and poet of the year in a few poetry competitions. She is inspired by the power of words, when it comes to transforming ourselves and our thoughts by the written word. She lives in Nashville, Tennessee with her two beautiful children.

Acknowledgement

I just wanna thank God for allowing me to
Live my dreams and for giving me such a beautiful gift
To share with others.
It starts with Him, and it will end with Him.
I feel truly blessed and honored by you.
You gave me this to use for influential purposes,
So I can spread the message of love, peace, unity and freedom.
I understand I am responsible for uplifting
And connecting with others around the world.

I also owe thanks to my beautiful mother
For putting up with me and loving me unconditionally.
You are the greatest person on earth to me.
I just wanna say thank you
For molding me to who I am today.
I wanna thank my kids' art teacher, Ms. Crenshaw,
For always giving me advice and always making sure
I stay focus and motivated on my goals.
I love you too, and you are such a sweet, beautiful person.
I am feel lucky to have met you and call you a friend of mine.

www.ingramcontent.com/pod-product-compliance
Lightning Source LLC
LaVergne TN
LVHW011206080426
835508LV00007B/630